Journey into a Black Hole

by Franklyn M. Branley
illustrated by Marc Simont

A Harper Trophy Book
Harper & Row, Publishers

The *Let's-Read-and-Find-Out Book*™ series was originated by Dr. Franklyn M. Branley, Astronomer Emeritus and former Chairman of the American Museum–Hayden Planetarium, and was formerly co-edited by him and Dr. Roma Gans, Professor Emeritus of Childhood Education, Teachers College, Columbia University. Text and illustrations for each of the more than 100 books in the series are checked for accuracy by an expert in the relevant field. The titles available in paperback are listed below. Look for them at your local bookstore or library.

JOURNEY INTO A BLACK HOLE
Text copyright © 1986 by Franklyn M. Branley
Illustrations copyright © 1986 by Marc Simont
Printed in Mexico
For information address Harper & Row Junior Books,
10 East 53rd Street, New York, N.Y. 10022.
Published in hardcover by Thomas Y. Crowell, New York.
First Harper Trophy edition, 1988.

Library of Congress Cataloging-in-Publication Data
Branley, Franklyn Mansfield, 1915-
  Journey into a black hole.

  (Let's-read-and-find-out-science book)
  Summary: Takes the reader on an imaginary journey
to a black hole.
  1. Black holes (Astronomy)—Juvenile literature.
[1. Black holes (Astronomy)] I. Simont, Marc, ill.
II. Title. III. Series.
QB843.B55B73 1986   523.8   85-48249
ISBN 0-690-04543-3
ISBN 0-690-04544-1 (lib. bdg.)

  (Let's-read-and-find-out book)
  (A Harper Trophy book)
ISBN 0-06-445075-9 (pbk.)

Journey into a Black Hole

Stars seem to last forever. But they don't.

The Sun is our star. It is much, much bigger than the Earth. It has been shining for 5 billion years. It will probably shine for another 5 billion years. That's a long, long time. But it is not forever. Stars are born, they last a long time, and then they die out.

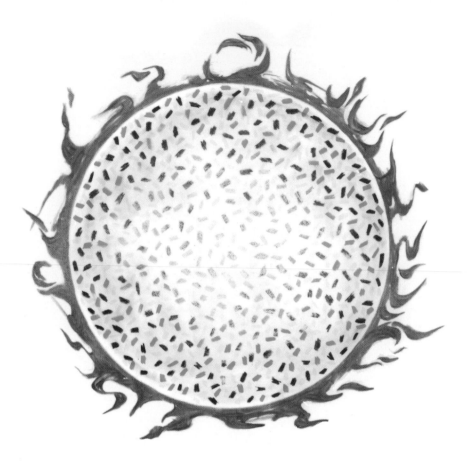

Stars are made of hot gases, mostly hydrogen and
helium. The gas particles are spread far apart. After a long
time, the gases cool. Then the stars collapse. Gravity

pulls the gases toward the center. The gases pack closer and closer together.

The gases in a star like the Sun may be packed into a space even smaller than the Earth.

Some stars contain a much greater amount of gases than the Sun. These stars have greater mass. A star with more mass than the Sun packs together more tightly. It becomes a black hole.

It is called a black hole because no light can escape from it. Material can go into it but can never come out. A black hole is more like a ball of gases packed together very tightly than it is like a hole.

I think I found one.

We cannot see a black hole, but we know it is there.

A black hole has strong gravity. It pulls on a nearby star. The star changes position as the black hole pulls on it. We can see this neighbor star. And we can see it move from side to side.

Strong X rays also tell us where there is a black hole. As gases are pulled toward a black hole, X rays are made just outside the hole itself. We can pick up those X rays with X-ray telescopes. So we have another clue to a black hole.

Suppose you could go to a black hole. What would happen? No one really knows. It would have to be a make-believe journey. We are sure no one could ever return, so it would be a one-way trip.

A ticket to a black hole?
That's a one-way trip.

After traveling a long, long time from Earth you would get close to a bright star called HDE 226868. It is millions of times brighter than the Sun. It is a large, blue star in Cygnus, the swan. That's a constellation we can see in the skies of summer.

19

You see gases stream away from the star and pulled into space. After swirling about, they form a stream that flows into a place close by. That's where the black hole is located. The gases give off X rays, and then they disappear. The black hole is pulling the star apart.

As you get closer to the black hole, gravity becomes
millions of times greater than gravity is on Earth. Strange
things begin to happen. Say you are moving feet first.
Gravity at your feet is much stronger than it is at your
head. Your feet are pulled more than your head because
they are closer to the black hole. You are stretched out.
Your body gets longer and longer, thinner and thinner.

A thousand miles from the black hole you would be very long, and then you would be pulled apart. But suppose that somehow you were able to stay together and move even closer.

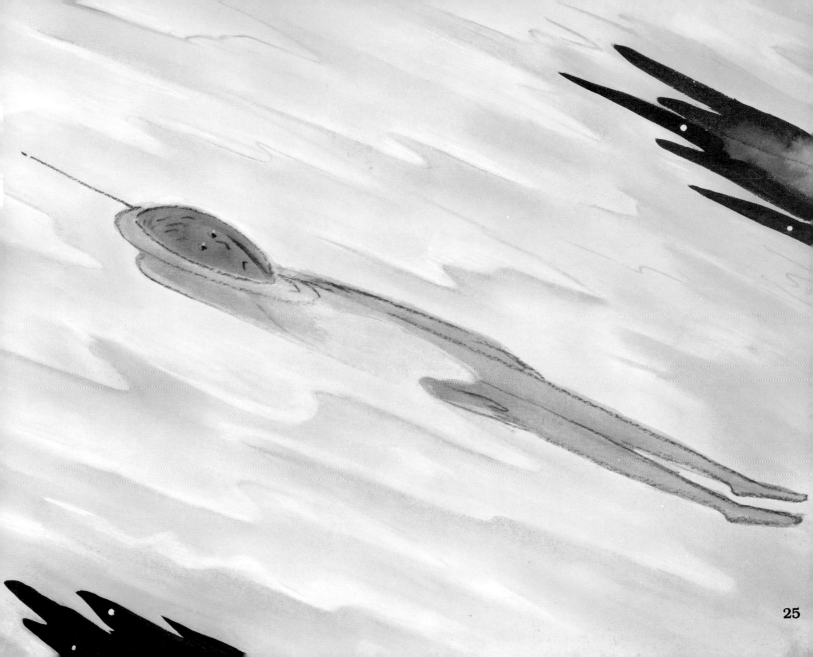

You move faster and faster toward the black hole. You reach the edge and are bombarded by X rays. All of a sudden you are over the edge and inside the black hole.

Gravity is so strong it pulls you apart. You become separate atoms. And the atoms are broken into pieces of atoms. You are packed into the hole with more and more gas from HDE 226868. There is so much gas and it is packed so tightly together, a single thimbleful weighs billions of tons.

Don't worry if you cannot imagine anything so heavy. No one can. It is incredible. Everything about black holes is incredible.

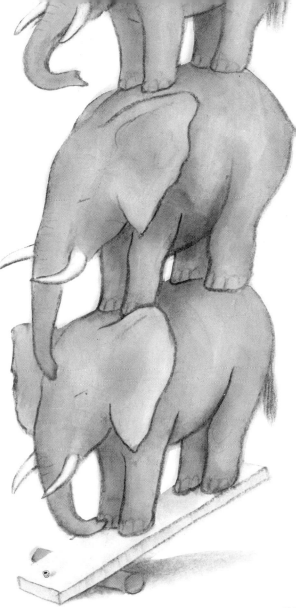

This is incredible!

I think I found another one.

We cannot prove there are black holes. But astronomers believe there may be billions of them. There may be great big ones, and also very small ones. Whenever a massive star collapses, it probably becomes a black hole. And stars have been collapsing for billions of years.

I changed my mind. I want a round-trip ticket to the Grand Canyon.

No one will ever be able to go to a black hole. No one would ever want to. But should anyone ever invite you on such a journey, don't go. It would be a one-way trip.